I0178116

# Women's Power Awakened

by

## Nadja

NadjaMedia.com

NadjaMedia.com

Nadja Media
530 Los Angeles Ave., Suite 115
Moorpark, California 93021

Cover art by Katrina Joyner

ISBN-10: 1942057091
ISBN-13: 978-1-942057-09-3

Copyright © 2010 by Nadja.

All rights reserved. No part of this book may be reproduced by any mechanical, photographic, or electronic process, or in the form of a phonographic recording; nor may it be stored in a retrieval system, transmitted, or otherwise be copied for public or private use— other than for "fair use" as brief quotations embodied in articles and reviews—without prior written permission of the publisher.

This is a work of fiction. Names, characters, places, and incidents either are a product of the author's imagination or are used fictitiously, and any resemblance to actual persons, living or dead, business establishments, events, or locales is entirely coincidental. No liability is assumed for damages resulting from the use of or misinterpretation of information contained herein. The information is meant as a guideline only and to help Humanity better reflect upon themselves, where they have been, where they are now, and where they potentially may be going. Nadja never advocates the use of violence in any form.

# Acknowledgments

Thank you to all the women from the beginning of history up to this point in time who have paved the way for our freedom today. The debt we owe them is to live our lives as fully developed, conscious Human Beings.

# Dedication

Written for the modern day woman who is
stepping into her full power.

❦

Women are the Flowers of the Earth. Through
them the world bears fruit.

# Introduction

Women have come into their own to take their rightful place as equal partners with their men. Read this to discover your authentic voice, your role, and your powerful Goddess energy. We can create divine partnerships where each gender cherishes and honors the other.

# Foreword

This book is written to free men and women everywhere and from all walks of life from their programmed roles and to encourage them to step past their conditioning and enter an era where all people can be free to be who they are and to develop their full potential. This book is also written in commemoration of all those women who were inspired to break out of the mold to bring their remarkable gifts of leadership, spirituality, science, letters, medicine, art, dance, business, and government to the Planet. In addition, this writing is brought forth in memory of those who were tortured and killed for daring to be themselves and speak their truth or who were murdered just because they were female. Last but not least, this book is written to honor all those women who endured and lived lives of "quiet desperation," while being steadfast in carrying out their duties; for others whose talents and careers were squelched or totally disregarded because of their gender; and for those who were happy and well adjusted being wonderful mothers, wives, and the hub of the family.

Of course, the author recognizes that there have been many men who, in spite of their cultural conditioning, truly loved, respected, and honored women. They understood that women were intellectually equal and capable of high achievement given the same educational and cultural opportunities as men. We thank them and are grateful for their wisdom and awareness and for being role models for men in the future.

# Women Mentors

Friend Jakki, Isadora Duncan, Emily Dickinson, Marie Curie, Joan of Ark, Hildegard de Bingen, Isak Dinesen, Sister Corita Kent, Mother Teresa, Saint Therese Little Flower, Amma, Esther, Dhyani Ywahoo, Kathie Kolwitz, Anne Frank, Ann Wigmore, Sulamith Wolfing, Maria Treben, Carla Emery, Maria Alice Campos Freer, Maureen Moss, Katheryn Kuhlman, Lucille Ball, Wanda Landowski, Oprah, Sally Fallon, SARK, Debbie Ford, Florence Nightingale, Olga Worrall, Sylvia Ashton Warner, Susun Weed, Corrie Ten Boom, Jill Bolte Taylor, Beatrix Potter, Rachel Carson, Inelia Benz, Dawn Clark, Dr. Sarah Larsen, Carol Tuttle, Jo Dunning, Debra Cummings, Anais

Ninn, Adele Davis, Esther Williams, Leslie Caron, Carol Burnett, Georgia O'Keeffe, Marian Anderson, Anna Pavlova, Julia Child, Annie Besant, Joan Baez, Maria Montessori, Jane Hull, Carolyn Keen, Wonder Woman, Laura Ingalls Wilder, Juliette Gordon Low, Audrey Hepburn, Betsy Ross, Enya, Edith Piaf, Yma Sumac, Brenda Starr, Ruth Stout, Christel Hughes, Princess Diana, Jackie Kennedy, Jennifer McLean, Donna Eden, Akiane Kramarik, Sherry Wilde, Elle Febbo. Christa McAuliffe, Margaret Meade, The International Council of Thirteen Indigenous Grandmothers, Joni Eareckson Tada, Harriet Tubman, Helen Keller, Amelia Earhart, Kateri Tekakwitha, Grandma Moses, Pearl Buck, Lynn Waldrop, Mary Hall, Jean Houston, Indra Devi, Jill Jackson, Melonie, Marianne Williamson, Claudia Gittens, Magenta Pixie, Andie DePass, Sophia Zoe, Aviva Gold, Shiloh Sophia, Poloma Aurea Dawn, Alexandra Meadors, Judy Cali, Helena Petrovna Blavatsky, and Peta Amber Lynne.

# Women's Power

# Awakened

A woman is a goddess

You'd better believe

Whatever she wants

She can always achieve

The feminine energy

Has come into power

Don't worry, Men,

And please don't cower

We won't treat you

Like you treated us

We'll honor and respect you

And let you drive the bus

The programmed roles

We were forced to play

Caused war between the sexes

And the mess we're in today

We'll hold you accountable

Yet we forgive

Please forgive us

Let go and let live

We love you, Men,

More than ever

Even though we're free

We don't want to be clever

We want to be sincere

And deal truthfully with you

As complete human beings

We love you through and through

What a relief

No more games

We don't have to pretend

We have no brains

To put women down

Was such a waste

The whole world suffered

But that was the case

Every human being

Has much to offer

To squelch one person without any reason

Is to diminish the world and commit treason

At last we have achieved

Full equality

We can change the world for better

And wait until you see

What changes we can make

When our wisdom is respected

How our dying world responds

Once it is corrected

The world will be gentler

With women at the helm

It will fill with love and kindness

And the angelic realm

Wars will disappear

No more sons will be killed

Creativity will flourish

Children's dreams will be fulfilled

People will count

Not money or greed

People will have

What they need

We'll respect human rights

Make sure they are upheld

Race, age, gender

Treated equally tender

The Industrial Revolution

Has seen its day

We will return to Mother Earth

To a Sacred Living Way

The homestead will flourish

No more harshness to dread

Men and women stay home

And raise their children instead

We can also be tough

We can see through a lie

Nothing can fool us

We can lead until we die

You can trust us to be fair

We will not gossip or emote

You can count on us

We will have a fair vote

No more lobbies

We will serve the people

Humanity will survive

And no longer be feeble

We'll distribute the goods

To people world wide

It will get to who needs it

Politics aside

We will serve the world fairly

Women's power at last

No more bullies

To screw up like the past

Women don't have

To be just like men

We can be our true selves

And still say when

We can be feminine

Cute and beautiful, too

Smart and delectable

And still rule

For the feminine spirit

This is the hour

To stand up strong

And take back our power

A woman who defines herself

By her husband's career

Is living slave mentality

Out of ignorance and fear

Some women marry

A money machine

When that runs dry

Poof goes the dream

If you marry just for money

And the well runs dry

You can only blame yourself

Please don't cry

When a couple goes to court

Money talks

The woman usually loses

And the man walks

Wait for the man

Who opens your heart

Nourishes your soul

And then never part

Abuse will be

A thing of the past

Women will be honored

For as long as we last

Men will be safe

They can relax

They can be their true selves

These are the facts

Men can feel

Men can be real

They don't have to lead

They can heal

The times weren't kind

To women and men

They were forced to play roles

That didn't fit them

Now is the time

When you can be you

Live in the moment

And know who's who

People are strong

Courageous and brave

The genders honor one another

This is how to behave

Women are liberated

We now have our power

We'll be fair to our men

This is our hour

No gender should conquer

The other to win

This isn't right

You know from within

To brainwash a woman

To become a slave

Is not the way

For a true man to behave

Women have raised you

From infancy on

Without their care

You would be long gone

Men know in their psyche

That women are stronger

They cannot lie to themselves

No, not any longer

For a woman to bear children

And raise them from birth

Is proof of the pudding

Of our strength and our worth

Motherhood is

A sacred duty

Done correctly

A Gift of Beauty

Women are equals

Open your eyes

We are strong and amazing

In spite of our size

Our strength is our feelings,

Our intuition, our heart

We are now freed

To play our true part

No longer must we be

Dependent slaves for men

We can rule the world

And make it thrive once again

Each gender needs

To pull their own weight

The world is so weary

All are needed to participate

Between men and women

A truce it will be

Let's be holy interdependent

So we can truly See

We can right the world

If we do this together

Planet Earth will become

An absolute treasure

No more manipulation

Of a woman's mind

No more taking advantage

Of the female kind

Men and Women let's unite

We have gone global

Let's make the world

At long last noble

# Final Words

"The day will come when men will recognize woman as his peer, not only at the fireside, but in councils of the nation. Then, and not until then, will there be the perfect comradeship, the ideal union between the sexes that shall result in the highest development of the race."

— Susan B. Anthony

# About The Author

After working many years in the public sector Nadja is reinventing herself as an artist and writer. She has an eclectic background. Her joys include adventuring on the Open Road, dancing, cooking, being in nature, writing and painting. She is also interested in natural building, organic gardening, alternative health, life-long learning, travel, and living moment to moment. Nadja writes for the conscious community and people who are interested in healing, meditation, transformation, ascension, and the New Earth. This includes highly sensitive people, Starseeds, Indigos, empaths, Light Workers, energy healers, artists, visionaries, and those in recovery and discovery.

# Resources

CenterForFoodSafety.org

FoodAndWaterWatch.org

Ienearth.org

CalixtoSuarez.com

Chanchka.com

RingingCedars.com

FoodBabe.com

Mercola.com

NaturalNews.com

Bioneers.org

WestonPrice.org

NextWorldTV.com

# Resources

**Crimes Against Nature** by Robert F. Kennedy

**Cosmic Ordering Made Easier** by Ellen Watts

M. T. Keshe

Santos Bonacci

Dr. Masaru Emoto

Vandana Shiva

Masanobu Fukuoka

Chunyi Lin

Susun Weed

Tusli Gabbard

Paul Stamets

Buckmaster Fuller

David Wilcock

Matt Kahn

# Resources

Lynn Waldrop

John Newton

Christel Hughes

Debora Wayne

Tarek Bibi

Lanna Spencer

Sophia Zoe

Jo Dunning

Lisa Transcendence Brown

Julie Renee

Eckhart Tolle

Neale Donald Walsch

Stacey Mayo

Dorian Light

# Resources

Lottie Cooper

Andie DePass

Judy Cali

Marianne Williamson

Dr. Madlena Kantscheff

Dipal Shah

Jenny Ngo

Emmanuel Dagher

Magenta Pixie

Jarrad Hewett

Tamra Oviatt

Cathy Hohmeyer

Morry Zelcovitch

Rassouli

# Resources

Akiane Kramarik

SARK

Shiloh Sophia

Aviva Gold

Ho'oponopono

**The Emotion Code** by Bradley Nelson

Emotional Freedom Technique (EFT)

Helpguide.org

Acim.org

Wopg.org

BirthingAndRebirthing.com

YouWealthRevolution.com

FromHeartacheToJoy.com

AcousticHealth.com

# Resources

GalacticConnection.com

NotesFromTheUniverse.com

Homeopathic Cell Salts

OptimumHealthInstitute.com

NewPhoenixRising.com

# Also By Nadja

Soft-cover books, eBooks, MP3s, and CDs, Smashwords, Amazon, Kindle, CreateSpace, CDBaby, iTunes, YouTube, and your local bookstore by request.

**River of Living Light**

**Evolution Revolution**

**Random Thoughts and Poems**

**Hopi Blue Corn**

**El Maiz Azul de los Hopis**

**Visionary Tales for the New Earth**

**Color Me Bright Coloring Book**

**Blue Sky**

Ascension Codes

Raps, Chants, and Rants

Women's Power Awakened

Ozzengoggle Poems

From the City of Shem

You Are Not Alone

Family Secrets

Flying Heart

Bullies

www.ingramcontent.com/pod-product-compliance
Lightning Source LLC
Chambersburg PA
CBHW070759050426
42452CB00012B/2402